United States
Department of
Agriculture

Forest Service

Southern
Research Station

Resource Bulletin
SRS–162

Florida Harvest and Utilization Study, 2008

James W. Bentley and
Tony G. Johnson

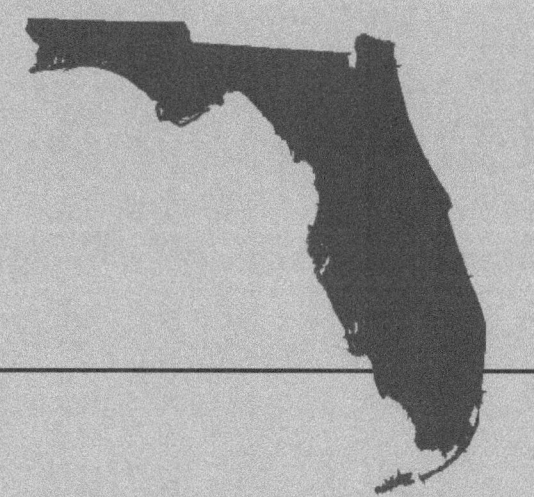

The Authors:

James W. Bentley, Resource Forester, and **Tony G. Johnson**, Resource Analyst, U.S. Forest Service, Southern Research Station, Knoxville, TN 37919.

September 2009

Southern Research Station
200 W.T. Weaver Blvd.
Asheville, NC 28804

Foreword

This resource bulletin describes the principal findings of a harvest and utilization study conducted during the eighth inventory of Florida's forest resources. Survey crews sampled and measured trees harvested in a variety of logging operations, and analysts calculated wood volume and percent of wood utilization. Harvest volume data and factors for growing-stock and nongrowing-stock logging residue are described and interpreted.

Annual surveys of America's forest resources are mandated by the Forest and Rangeland Act of 1978. Surveys and utilization studies are part of a continuing, nationwide undertaking by regional experiment stations of the Forest Service, U.S. Department of Agriculture. Inventories and utilization studies of the 13 Southern States (Alabama, Arkansas, Florida, Georgia, Kentucky, Louisiana, Mississippi, North Carolina, Oklahoma, South Carolina, Tennessee, Texas, and Virginia) and the Commonwealth of Puerto Rico are conducted by the Southern Research Station, Forest Inventory and Analysis (FIA) Research Work Unit. Unit headquarters is in Knoxville, TN, and FIA has operational offices in Asheville, NC, and Starkville, MS. The primary objective of these appraisals is to develop and maintain resource information needed to formulate sound forest policies and programs. More information about Forest Service resource inventories is available in "The Enhanced Forest Inventory and Analysis Program—National Sampling Design and Estimation Procedures" (Bechtold and Patterson 2005).

Tabular data included in FIA resource bulletins present a comprehensive array of forest resource statistics, but additional information is available to those who require more specific information. Access to data for the Southern States can be found at: http://srsfia2.fs.fed.us/data/index.shtml.

Acknowledgments

The authors thank Britt Evans and Jarek Nowak for their review and comments; Anne Jenkins, Janet Griffin, Carolyn Steppleton, and Sharon Johnson for the map, tables, graphs, and statistical checking; and the Southern Research Station (SRS) Technical Publications Team for editorial review, styling, and publication of this report.

The SRS gratefully acknowledges the cooperation and assistance of the Florida Department of Agriculture and Consumer Services, Division of Forestry, in collecting harvest and utilization data. Appreciation is also extended to forest industry and loggers for allowing access to their land and logging operations.

Contents

[a] All tables in this report are available in Microsoft® Excel workbook files. Upon request, these files will be supplied in the format the customer requests.

The use of trade or firm names in this publication is for reader information and does not imply endorsement by the U.S. Department of Agriculture of any product or service.

Figure 1—Harvest operations, Florida, 2008.

Florida Harvest and Utilization Study, 2008

James W. Bentley and Tony G. Johnson

Introduction

Forest planners and managers have a continuing need for information about the timber resource, and the general public is expressing increasing interest in the effects of logging. Therefore, up-to-date data on the Nation's forests—and how the forests are changing—are essential to well informed decisionmaking. Information about the condition of and changes in the timber resource of Florida comes from three primary sources: (1) inventory plots, which describe current conditions and quantify changes due to mortality, growth, removals, and land use; (2) mill surveys, which quantify timber volume harvested and delivered to primary wood products facilities, i.e., sawmills, pulpmills, veneer mills, composite panel mills, and pole mills; and (3) logging utilization studies, which characterize harvest operations and quantify the timber volume that is cut and utilized, and that portion that is left in the forest.

This bulletin presents the findings of a 2008 harvest and utilization study in Florida. The study's main goal was to provide an estimate of softwood and hardwood volume used, and of volume left in the woods as logging residue. Survey crews randomly selected and measured felled trees on 82 active harvest operations throughout Florida (fig. 1). This bulletin also provides information on logging in Florida and some general characteristics of trees harvested for various products, examples of which are average diameter at breast height (d.b.h.) by product, average bole length by product, average heights of residual stumps, and average diameter outside bark (d.o.b.) at the end of utilization.

Some standard Forest Inventory and Analysis (FIA) terms are used in this study. Two of particular importance for understanding and interpreting study results are growing stock and nongrowing stock. A growing-stock tree is a live tree of commercial species that either contains or is capable of producing at least one 12-foot or two 8-foot logs in the saw-log portion of the bole. A nongrowing-stock tree is one that does not meet the requirements of growing stock due to poor form or rot. For growing-stock trees, the growing-stock portion of a tree (5-inches d.b.h. or larger) includes the volume of sound wood between a 1-foot stump and a 4-inch top, d.o.b. Volume in the 1-foot stump, volume in the main stem from 4 inches to the growing top of the tree, and the volume of any limbs 4 inches or larger with at least one 5-foot section are considered nongrowing-stock volume by FIA standards. Rough or rotten trees were also sampled and make up another piece of nongrowing-stock (cull) volume. Figure 2 illustrates a poletimber tree, a sawtimber tree, and the growing-stock section of each.

Methods

Site Stratification and Selection

Producing a complete list of timber-harvesting operations and ownerships in a State such as Florida is problematic. Because of the complexity of the timber industry, it is impossible to list the names and locations of all during the timeframe considered in this resource bulletin. Many uncontrollable factors affect how, when, and where harvesting operations take place, but the most common events that affect harvesting operations are weather and timber markets. A random sample provides a reasonably accurate estimate of utilization.

The sites selected for study were stratified by species group and product using the most recent data available for county-level output of timber products harvested in Florida by species group (Johnson and others 2008). Using those proportions, we designated 62 of the 82 selected sites as softwood operations and the remaining 20 as hardwood operations. We used the same guidelines to designate harvest operations by product but allowed more flexibility because

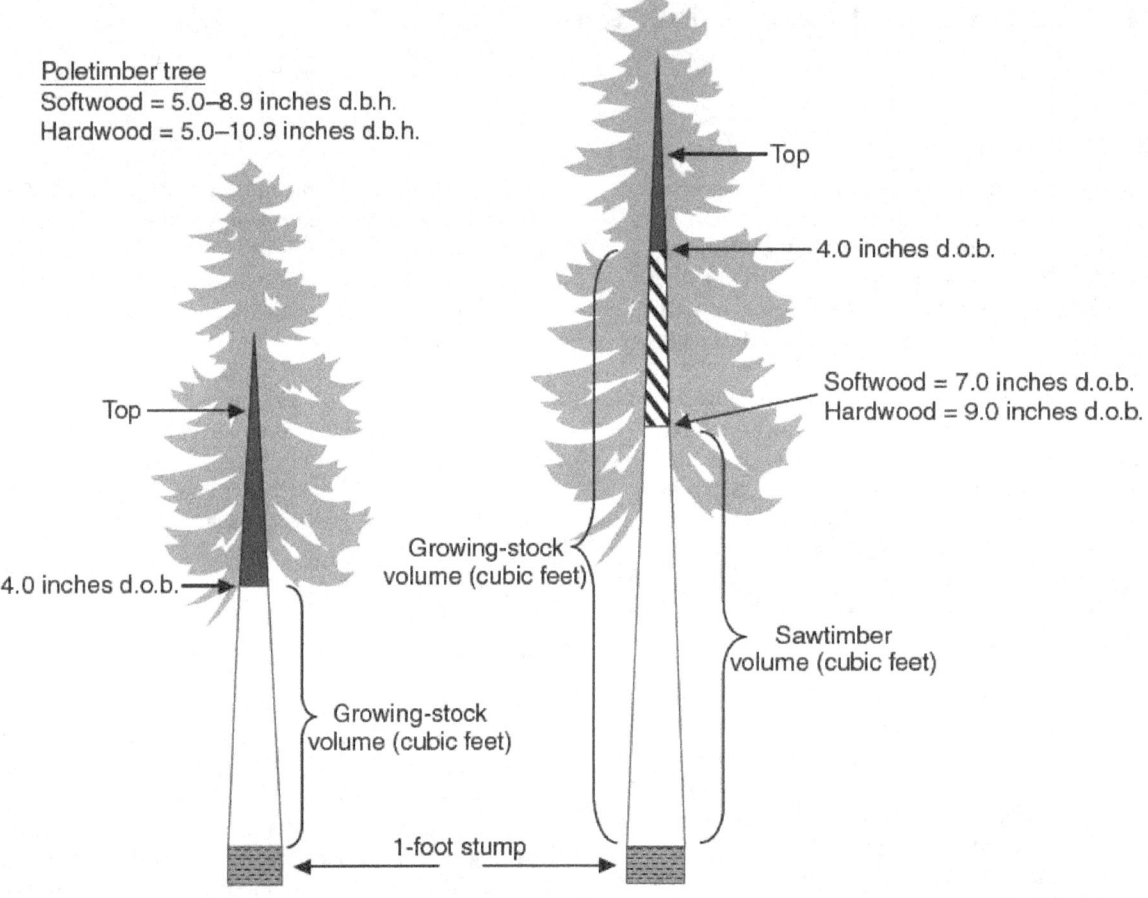

Sawtimber tree
Softwood = at least 9.0 inches d.b.h.
Hardwood = at least 11.0 inches d.b.h.

Poletimber tree
Softwood = 5.0–8.9 inches d.b.h.
Hardwood = 5.0–10.9 inches d.b.h.

Top

4.0 inches d.o.b.

Softwood = 7.0 inches d.o.b.
Hardwood = 9.0 inches d.o.b.

Top

4.0 inches d.o.b.

Growing-stock
volume (cubic feet)

Sawtimber
volume (cubic feet)

Growing-stock
volume (cubic feet)

1-foot stump

Figure 2—Stem sections of poletimber and sawtimber trees.

of the difficulty in locating harvesting operations for some products. Table 1 shows the final breakdown number of harvest operations, total trees, trees planted, and percentage of trees planted by product and species group.

After the harvest operations were stratified by major species group and product, the operations were placed in the appropriate region and county in the State. Using county-level product output data (Johnson and others 2008) and a map showing current mill locations, prospective utilization sites were selected based on a high probability of locating a harvesting operation for the particular product and species group assigned. Figure 1 shows where the final harvest operations considered in this bulletin were located.

Data Collection

During the eighth survey, field crews were trained to collect data on felled trees at harvest locations. Using the list of operations and a map of sites, they began collecting data by county for the particular species group and designated product(s). Data were collected from July 2008 to November 2008 on active harvest operations. To locate active harvest sites, field crews visited local mills and consulted county personnel.

At each harvest operation site, field crews talked to the logger or person in charge of operations. These contacts provided vital information about product(s) utilized,

Table 1—Number of operations, total trees, planted trees, and percent planted by product and species group, Florida, 2008

Product and species group	Operations	Trees Total	Trees Planted	
		- - - - - - - number - - - - - - -		percent
Saw logs				
Softwood	16	420	211	50
Hardwood	7	101	0	—
Total	23	521	211	40
Veneer logs				
Softwood	8	169	58	34
Hardwood	0	0	0	—
Total	8	169	58	34
Composite panels				
Softwood	4	91	91	100
Hardwood	0	0	0	—
Total	4	91	91	100
Pulpwood				
Softwood	13	481	403	84
Hardwood	10	263	22	8
Total	23	744	425	57
Poles/pilings				
Softwood	4	83	58	71
Hardwood	0	0	0	—
Total	4	83	58	71
Fence posts				
Softwood	4	84	59	70
Hardwood	0	0	0	—
Total	4	84	59	70
Fuelwood				
Softwood	4	96	78	81
Hardwood	3	72	72	100
Total	7	168	150	89
Mulch				
Softwood	9	246	91	9
Hardwood	0	8	0	—
Total	9	254	91	9
All products				
Softwood	62	1,670	1,049	63
Hardwood	20	444	94	21
Total	82	2,114	1,143	54

— = no sample for the cell.

specific diameters, and log lengths the receiving mill(s) would accept, along with minimum diameters at the cutoff points for specific products. Additional information about the logging crew was noted, such as type and amount of equipment they used as well as age of the equipment, number of loads hauled per day, certifications of the loggers, and distances they were willing to travel for work. This information was used to determine the level of mechanization for each harvesting operation.

The goal of the field crew, at each harvest operation site, was to measure 25 to 30 trees for each product. This number ensured an adequate representation of overutilization and underutilization for a given type of harvest operation. Trees were randomly selected and had to be at least 5 inches d.b.h. and alive prior to harvest. Although often bucked, limbed, and topped, the main bole of each tree selected for measurement had to be intact to be measured for utilization. The State, unit, county, and location number were recorded for each site. Each tree was assigned a number and identified by species, d.b.h., tree class, product, bole length, and percentage of cull (if rot was detected). Each tree was measured from the top of the cut stump to the end of utilization. Measurements were made along the main stem in sections no longer than 16 feet until the end of utilization. The end of utilization usually is determined by the sawyer, according to particular specifications set by the receiving mill(s). FIA merchantability standards for growing-stock volume are defined as the volume in the main stem of the tree from a 1-foot stump to a 4-inch top. However, most trees are not cut exactly at a 1-foot stump, nor are they cut off at exactly 4 inches. For example, trees cut off above a 1-foot stump and below 4 inches would be considered underutilized, and that volume not utilized would be considered growing-stock residue. On the other hand, by FIA standards, trees cut below a 1-foot stump and above a 4-inch top are considered 100 percent utilized, and those portions below and above are considered overutilization. A myriad of combinations actually occur on active harvest operations. The aggregated volume from measured trees has provided overutilization and underutilization factors that can be applied to statewide inventory results for an estimate of growing-stock and nongrowing-stock logging residues. Other required measurements, besides d.b.h. and end of utilization, are the top of the sawtimber portion (7.0 inches in softwoods and 9.0 inches in hardwoods). Those measurements allow calculation of the sawtimber and poletimber portion of the growing-stock section.

Highlights

Characteristics of Harvested Trees in Florida

Results of this study identify several key characteristics of trees harvested. Such findings cannot be obtained from a typical field inventory or a forest industry study that supplies product output data only. Characteristics such as average d.b.h. by product, average bole length by product, average residual stump height, and average d.o.b. at the end of utilization is vital information for a full understanding of the complex nature of removals. Averages discussed in this section are based on the measurement of 2,114 trees, of which 1,670 (79 percent) were softwood and 444 (21 percent) hardwood.

According to Johnson and others (2008), softwood and hardwood saw-log volume together accounted for 37 percent of the total product output for the State. The study classified 420 trees as having softwood saw logs averaging 10.9 inches d.b.h. Fifty percent, or 211 trees, were classified as planted softwood saw logs averaging 10.0 inches d.b.h., nearly 2 inches smaller than natural softwood saw logs averaging 11.9 inches d.b.h. It classified 101 hardwood trees as having saw logs averaging 18.6 inches d.b.h. Veneer and plywood constitute another component of the product mix for Florida. Based on 169 trees measured for softwood veneer, the average d.b.h. was 13.2 inches. Advances in lathe technology at softwood plywood mills are resulting in a drop of the average d.b.h. of peeler logs across the South. As expected, the d.b.h. of trees measured for pulpwood and composite panels was significantly smaller. Of the 481 softwood pulpwood trees measured, the average d.b.h. was 7.1 inches, while the 263 trees measured for hardwood

pulpwood averaged 8.4 inches d.b.h. Eighty-four percent, or 403 trees, of the softwood pulpwood trees were planted, averaging 6.7 inches d.b.h., slightly over 2 inches less than trees that come from natural stands. Ninety-one trees, all coming from planted stands, were measured for softwood composite panels averaging 6.7 inches d.b.h. Another component of the product mix is softwood mulch averaging 9.9 inches d.b.h. Table 2 shows the breakdown of average d.b.h. for each product by species group and stand origin.

Bole length is the distance between a 1-foot stump and a 4-inch top. As expected, trees harvested for solid wood products tended to have longer average bole lengths than trees harvested for pulpwood or composite panel products. The average bole length for softwood trees measured for saw logs was 56 feet, while trees measured for hardwood saw logs had an average bole length of 70 feet. In comparison, trees measured for pulpwood had average bole lengths of 34 feet for softwoods and 35 feet for hardwoods. Softwood veneer trees had an average bole length of 65 feet. Planted sites constituted a subset of all trees measured. Trees measured in planted stands tended to have shorter bole lengths than those measured in the natural stands. Table 3 shows the average bole length by species group, stand origin, and product.

Residual stump height is a key component in determining utilization rates for harvested trees. By FIA standards, the stump is that portion of the tree measured at ground level from the uphill side of the tree to 1 foot up the bole. Loggers try to maximize volume harvested by cutting the tree as close to the ground as possible. Residual stump heights

Table 2—Average diameter at breast height by species group, stand origin, and product, Florida, 2008

Species group and stand origin	Product							
	Saw logs	Veneer logs	Composite panels	Pulp-wood	Poles/ pilings	Fence posts	Fuel-wood	Mulch
	inches							
Softwood								
Natural	11.92	14.02	—	8.78	14.39	8.04	6.27	11.66
Planted	10.01	11.69	6.66	6.71	10.68	7.38	4.31	6.81
Total	10.96	13.22	6.66	7.05	11.76	7.58	4.67	9.87
Hardwood								
Natural	18.56	—	—	8.44	—	—	—	7.39
Planted	—	—	—	8.20	—	—	8.43	—
Total	18.56	—	—	8.42	—	—	8.43	7.39

— = no sample for the cell.

Table 3—Average bole length by species group, stand origin, and product, Florida, 2008

Species group and stand origin	Saw logs	Veneer logs	Composite panels	Pulpwood	Poles/ pilings	Fence posts	Fuel- wood	Mulch
				feet				
Softwood								
Natural	57.73	69.21	—	43.63	83.75	34.52	27.33	44.36
Planted	53.69	58.28	29.90	31.55	59.83	33.85	22.03	26.48
Total	55.70	65.46	29.90	33.51	66.83	34.05	23.02	37.75
Hardwood								
Natural	70.25	—	—	34.86	—	—	—	29.13
Planted	—	—	—	33.91	—	—	35.15	—
Total	70.25	—	—	34.78	—	—	35.15	29.13

— = no sample for the cell.

across the products ranged from 0.26 to 0.58 feet; however, most softwood trees harvested had an average residual stump height of about a 0.40 foot, while harvested hardwood trees averaged slightly higher residual stumps. In softwoods and across all products, this accounted for about 36 percent of the stump volume being utilized. In hardwoods and across all products, about 33 percent of stump volume was used. Stump volume for both hardwood and softwood contributed to utilization of the nongrowing-stock portion of trees, i.e., overutilization. Residual stump heights for trees coming from natural stands appear slightly higher than residual stump heights in planted stands. Table 4 shows the average residual stump heights for each product by species group.

The final component we used to determine use rates was d.o.b. at the end of utilization. Tops and limbs constitute most of the nongrowing-stock volume; they accounted for 52 percent of the nongrowing-stock portion that was utilized. The average end of utilization for softwood saw logs was 3.2 inches, and for hardwood saw logs 5.8 inches. The average end of utilization for softwood and hardwood pulpwood was 2.6 and 3.5 inches, respectively. Trees coming from natural and planted stands showed no difference in the end of utilization. Table 5 shows the average end of utilization by species group, stand origin, and product.

Table 4—Average residual stump height by species group, stand origin, and product, Florida, 2008

Species group and stand origin	Saw logs	Veneer logs	Composite panels	Pulp- wood	Poles/ pilings	Fence posts	Fuel- wood	Mulch
				feet				
Softwood								
Natural	0.56	0.38	—	0.51	0.58	0.50	0.45	0.45
Planted	0.41	0.46	0.26	0.33	0.38	0.30	0.36	0.53
Total	0.48	0.40	0.26	0.36	0.44	0.36	0.38	0.43
Hardwood								
Natural	0.58	—	—	0.58	—	—	—	0.43
Planted	—	—	—	0.31	—	—	0.34	—
Total	0.58	—	—	0.56	—	—	0.34	0.43

— = no sample for the cell.

Table 5—Average end of utilization by species group, stand origin, and product, Florida, 2008

Species group and stand origin	Product							
	Saw logs	Veneer logs	Composite panels	Pulp-wood	Poles/ pilings	Fence posts	Fuel-wood	Mulch
	inches							
Softwood								
Natural	3.31	3.46	—	2.73	4.65	2.20	2.11	3.18
Planted	3.03	3.28	2.17	2.58	2.93	2.51	1.87	2.05
Total	3.17	3.40	2.17	2.60	3.44	2.42	1.97	2.76
Hardwood								
Natural	5.76	—	—	3.53	—	—	—	3.48
Planted	—	—	—	3.06	—	—	—	—
Total	5.76	—	—	3.49	—	—	—	3.48

— = no sample for the cell.

Characteristics of Logging in Florida

When field crews visited the 82 individual logging operations, they asked the logger some additional questions. The purpose for these questions was two-fold: to predict the level of mechanization and to better understand a typical logging operation.

The information gathered provided data on the equipment loggers used and how they used it. Across the 82 operations, the average age of logging equipment in use was 5.6 years old, ranging from 1.5 to 20 years. Typically, at each logging operation, one rubber-tired feller-buncher with a sawhead was used for cutting down the trees. Skidding was accomplished with an average of a little more than one rubber-tired grapple skidder. Most of the delimbing was done on the landing with a pull-through delimber or near the landing with a push-through, gate style delimber. The trees were typically loaded with a knuckleboom loader averaging one loader per operation.

Field crews also noted hauling practices and productivity. The self-reported productivity ranged from 1 to 31 loads per day, averaging 9.7 loads per day across the State. An adequate number of double-bunk or pole trailers were most commonly used for hauling. Accounting for some sites being right beside a public road to others being miles away, the average distance from a public road to the logging site was 1.5 miles.

Field crews further noted preferences and characteristics of the loggers themselves. Most of the loggers were willing to travel as far as a neighboring county to work, but 21 of the 82 were willing to travel an average of 71 miles to work. Some Florida loggers procure wood for themselves, but most prefer working as contractors for forest industry or private timber buyers. All of the loggers in Florida were required to be certified, and most were members of a professional logger program.

Softwood Removals

Results from this study document 27,941 cubic feet of softwood volume, of which 23,716 cubic feet, or 85 percent, was used for product(s). Fifteen percent, or 4,225 cubic feet, was left onsite as logging residue (fig. 3). Thirty-three percent of the residue volume came from the growing-stock portion of the tree, while 67 percent came from the nongrowing-stock portion (stumps, tops, and limbs) (fig. 4) (table A.1).

The total softwood growing-stock volume measured was 24,011 cubic feet, of which 94 percent was utilized and 6 percent was logging residue (fig. 5). By FIA merchantability standards, the logging residue portion of growing-stock trees is underutilized volume. Of the total utilized volume, 1,118 cubic feet, or 4.7 percent, was from the nongrowing-stock portion of trees. By the same merchantability standards, that volume is considered overutilization (tables A.2 and A.3).

Softwood volumes and percentages are broken down further by poletimber and sawtimber, and by the various products measured (tables A.2 through A.9). By product, trees harvested for pulpwood and composite panels had above-average rates of utilization for the merchantable portion of the tree (97 percent) and the highest rates of overutilization (10.9 and 16.8 percent, respectively), meaning that more of the nongrowing-stock portion of the tree was used for product(s) and less was left as logging residue.

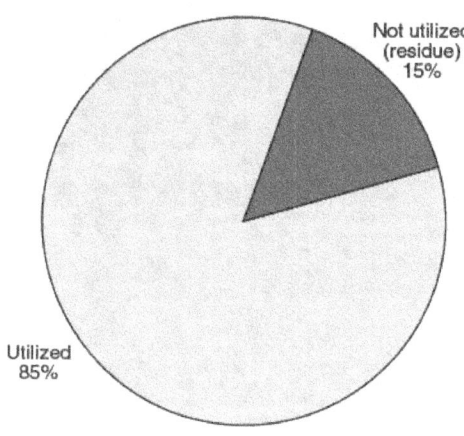

Total 27.9 thousand cubic feet

Figure 3—Disposition of total softwood harvest volume, Florida, 2008.

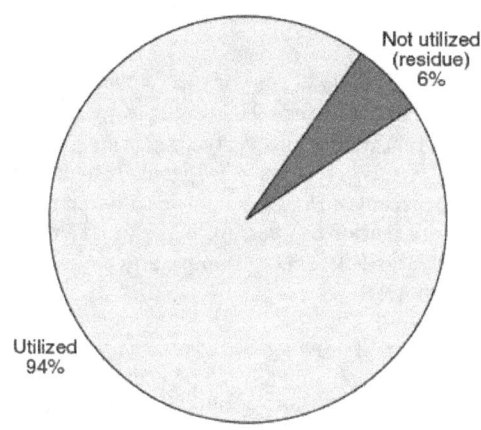

Total 24.0 thousand cubic feet

Figure 5—Disposition of softwood growing-stock volume, Florida, 2008.

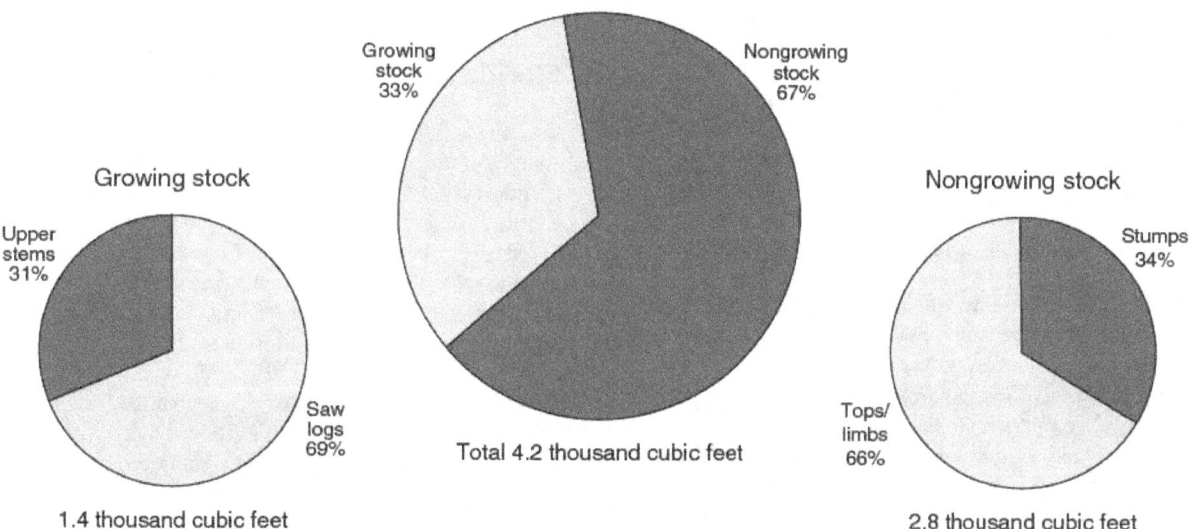

Figure 4—Softwood residue by volume type, Florida, 2008.

Softwood percentages and volumes presented in these tables represent only trees measured in this study of 82 active harvest operations. However, it is possible to apply the percentages to inventory data from Florida's eighth survey[1] to get an estimate of total softwood logging residues for the State. Annual softwood removal from all-live trees was 465.0 million cubic feet. Softwood growing-stock removals were 461.3 million cubic feet, or 99.2 percent of the total. Applying the factors from this study to total softwood removals for all-live trees tallied in the State survey provides an estimate of 90.7 million cubic feet total annual softwood residue. Of the total residue for all-live trees, 29.5 million cubic feet, or 33 percent, was considered growing-stock residue. The remaining 67 percent, or 61.2 million cubic feet, was nongrowing-stock residue from stumps, tops, and limbs, and cull trees not used.

[1] Brown, Mark J., Forester. Florida's Forests, 2007. Manuscript in preparation. Author can be reached at U.S. Department of Agriculture Forest Service, Southern Research Station, Forest Inventory and Analysis, 4700 Old Kingston Pike, Knoxville, TN 37919.

Hardwood Removals

Results from this study document 12,214 cubic feet of hardwood volume, of which 9,026 cubic feet, or 74 percent, was utilized for product(s). Twenty-six percent, or 3,188 cubic feet, was left onsite as logging residue (fig. 6). Forty-eight percent of residue volume came from the growing-stock portion of trees, and 52 percent came from the nongrowing-stock portion (stumps, tops, and limbs) (fig. 7) (table A.1).

The total hardwood growing-stock volume measured was 10,166 cubic feet, of which 85 percent was used and 15 percent was logging residue (fig. 8). By FIA merchantability standards, the logging residue portion is underutilized volume. Of the total utilized volume, 403 cubic feet, or 4.47 percent, was from the nongrowing-stock portion of trees. By the same merchantability standards, that volume is considered overutilization (tables A.10 and A.11).

Hardwood volumes and percentages also were measured for poletimber and sawtimber, and differentiated by the various products they provided (tables A.10 through A.17). At 90 percent, however, those trees measured for pulpwood were more fully utilized, and more of the nongrowing-stock portion was used for pulpwood. Trees measured for hardwood saw logs were the least utilized of all, although they have the most nongrowing-stock material.

Hardwood percentages and volumes presented in the tables represent only trees measured in this study of 82 active harvest operations. However, it is possible to apply the percentages to inventory data from Florida's eighth survey (see footnote 1 on page 7) to provide an estimate of total hardwood logging residue for the State. Annual hardwood removals from all-live trees totaled 123.2 million cubic feet. Hardwood growing-stock removals totaled 92.9 million cubic feet, or 75 percent of that total. Applying factors from this study to total hardwood removals from all-live trees tallied in the State survey provided an estimate of 38.6 million cubic feet total annual hardwood residue. Of that total, 17.9 million cubic feet, or 46 percent, was considered growing-stock residue. The remaining 54 percent, or 20.8 million cubic feet, was nongrowing-stock residue from stumps, tops and limbs, and rough or rotten trees that were not used.

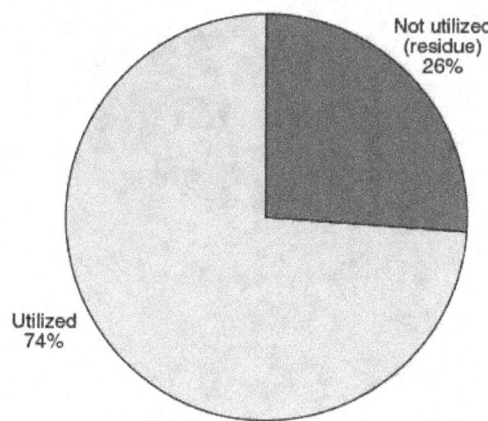

Total 12.2 thousand cubic feet

Figure 6—Disposition of total hardwood harvest volume, Florida, 2008.

Florida's Potential Biomass Availability

Logging residue has long been viewed as a possible source for bioenergy and other timber products, although traditionally it has not had any merchantable value. Retrieval of logging residue is a matter of economics, based on markets and demand. If markets are available and a willingness to pay a reasonable price exists, then more total tree volume is utilized for products. With this in mind, logging residue volume in Florida for 2002–2007, or the eighth survey, amounted to 129.3 million cubic feet, or 4.6 million green tons. Softwoods accounted for 70 percent, or 90.7 million cubic feet (3.2 million tons), of the logging residues, while 38.6 million cubic feet (1.5 million tons) came from hardwood species. Logging residue from the merchantable portion of all-live tree removals totaled 55.9 million cubic feet (2.0 million tons), or 43 percent of the total logging residue. Other sources accounted for 73.4 million cubic feet (2.6 million tons), or 57 percent of the total logging residue. Trees < 5 inches contributed another 3.1 million tons of possible logging residue. Tables 6 and 7 express the volume of timber removals by removals class, species group, and source in million cubic feet and green tons.

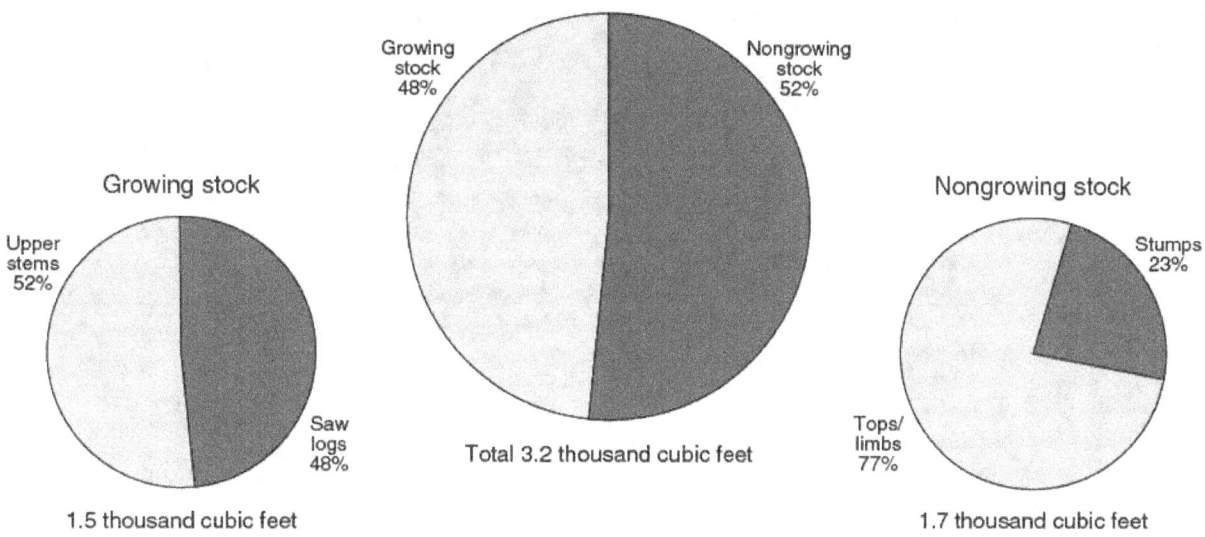

Growing stock

Upper
stems
52%

Saw
logs
48%

1.5 thousand cubic feet

Growing
stock
48%

Nongrowing
stock
52%

Total 3.2 thousand cubic feet

Nongrowing stock

Stumps
23%

Tops/
limbs
77%

1.7 thousand cubic feet

Figure 7—Hardwood residue by volume type, Florida, 2008.

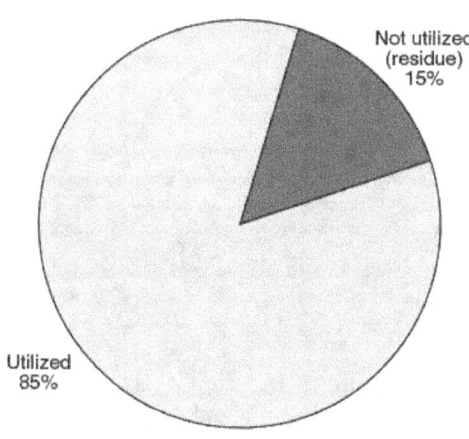

Not utilized
(residue)
15%

Utilized
85%

Total 10.2 thousand cubic feet

Figure 8—Disposition of hardwood growing-stock volume, Florida, 2008.

Over the same period, the area of timber harvested annually in Florida amounted to 330,900 acres, of which 190,600 acres (58 percent) underwent a final harvest, while 69,100 acres (21 percent) had a partial harvest and 61,900 acres (19 percent) had commercial thinning. The removals volume attributed to timber products and logging residues are directly related to these treated acres. Based on these estimates, we can say that 68.9 tons per acre in the merchantable and nonmerchantable portion of trees > 5 inches d.b.h were removed annually from Florida's timberland. Of the nearly 69 tons removed, 55.0 tons per acre were utilized for products, while 12.6 tons per acre were left as logging residue, excluding the residual stump. Assuming a 20-percent recovery rate for trees < 5 inches d.b.h., an additional 1.9 tons per acre was added, bringing the total logging residue to 14.7 tons per acre. This volume of logging residue is equivalent to a little more than one-half of a tree-length trailer load of wood for every acre treated in Florida.

Most loggers are very well equipped to handle the main bole or merchantable portion of the tree and even long, straight sections of forks or major limbs. However, a more

Table 6—Volume of timber removals by removals class, species group, and source, Florida, 2008

Removals class and species group	All sources	Source	
		All-live removals	Other sources
	million cubic feet		
Roundwood products			
Softwood	459.9	410.0	49.9
Hardwood	58.8	52.1	6.7
Total	518.7	462.1	56.6
Logging residues			
Softwood	90.7	30.1	60.6
Hardwood	38.6	25.8	12.8
Total	129.3	55.9	73.4
Other removals			
Softwood	31.2	24.9	6.3
Hardwood	56.5	45.2	11.3
Total	87.7	70.1	17.5
Total removals			
Softwood	581.7	465.0	116.8
Hardwood	153.9	123.2	30.8
Total	735.6	588.1	147.5

Numbers in rows and columns may not sum to totals due to rounding.

Table 7—Volume of timber removals by removals class, species group, and source, Florida, 2008

Removals class and species group	All sources	Source	
		All-live removals	Other sources
	green tons		
Roundwood products			
Softwood	16,000,015	14,264,473	1,735,542
Hardwood	2,209,330	1,958,925	250,405
Total	18,209,345	16,223,398	1,985,947
Logging residues			
Softwood	3,155,455	1,045,765	2,109,690
Hardwood	1,450,147	969,358	480,789
Total	4,605,602	2,015,123	2,590,479
Other removals			
Softwood	1,084,070	866,449	217,621
Hardwood	2,122,067	1,698,038	424,029
Total	3,206,137	2,564,487	641,650
Total removals			
Softwood	20,239,540	16,176,687	4,062,853
Hardwood	5,781,544	4,626,321	1,155,223
Total	26,021,084	20,803,008	5,218,076

effective way to handle rough trees with crooked boles, tops, and limbs is to chip this material at the site and transport the material in chip vans. Whole trees and portions of trees chipped onsite have a very limited use for industrial timber products. About the only use for this material is as mulch or boiler fuel. Bioenergy and mulch markets are particularly cost-efficient means of dealing with small trees < 5 inches d.b.h, as well as with rough and rotten trees and the nonmerchantable portions of growing-stock trees. Current literature suggests that, with conventional logging equipment, a 60-percent recovery rate is a realistic goal for possible extraction of formerly unutilized material (Perlack and others 2005). At this recovery rate, an additional 8.6 tons per acre of material once classified as logging residue could be added to the volume going for timber products.

Literature Cited

Bechtold, W.A.; Patterson, P.L., eds. 2005. The enhanced forest inventory and analysis program—national sampling design and estimation procedures. Gen. Tech. Rep. SRS–80. Asheville, NC: U.S. Department of Agriculture Forest Service, Southern Research Station. 85 p.

Johnson, T.G.; Bentley, J.W.; Howell, M. 2008. Florida's timber industry—an assessment of timber product output and use, 2005. Resour. Bull. SRS–133. Asheville, NC: U.S. Department of Agriculture Forest Service, Southern Research Station. 31 p.

Perlack, R.D.; Wright, L.L.; Turhollow, A. [and others]. 2005. Biomass as feedstock for a bioenergy and bioproducts industry: the technical feasibility of a billion-ton annual supply. ORNL/TM-2005/66. Washington, DC: U.S. Department of Energy and U.S. Department of Agriculture Forest Service. 73 p.

Glossary

Board foot. Unit of measure applied to roundwood. It relates to lumber that is 1-foot long, 1-foot wide, and 1-inch thick (or its equivalent).

Composite products. Roundwood products manufactured into chips, wafers, strands, flakes, shavings, or sawdust and then reconstituted into a variety of panel and engineered lumber products.

Drain. The volume of roundwood removed from any geographic area where timber is grown.

Growing-stock removals. The growing-stock volume removed from poletimber and sawtimber trees in the timberland inventory. (Note: Includes volume removed for roundwood products, logging residues, and other removals.)

Growing-stock trees. Living trees of commercial species classified as sawtimber, poletimber, saplings, and seedlings. Growing-stock trees must contain at least one 12-foot or two 8-foot logs in the saw-log portion, currently or potentially (if too small to qualify). The log(s) must meet dimension and merchantability standards and have, currently or potentially, one-third of the gross board-foot volume in sound wood.

Growing-stock volume. The cubic-foot volume of sound wood in growing-stock trees at least 5.0 inches d.b.h. from a 1-foot stump to a minimum 4.0-inch top d.o.b. of the central stem.

Hardwoods. Dicotyledonous trees, usually broadleaf and deciduous.

Soft hardwoods. Hardwood species with an average specific gravity of 0.50 or less, such as gums, yellow-poplar, cottonwoods, red maple, basswoods, and willows.

Hard hardwoods. Hardwood species with an average specific gravity > 0.50, such as oaks, hard maples, hickories, and beech.

Industrial roundwood products. Any primary use of the main stem of a tree, such as saw logs, pulpwood, and veneer logs, intended to be processed into primary wood products, such as lumber, wood pulp, and sheathing, at primary wood-using mills.

International ¼-inch rule. A log rule or formula for estimating the board-foot volume of logs, allowing ½-inch of taper for each 4-foot length. The rule appears in a number of forms that allow for kerf. In the form used by FIA, a ¼-inch of kerf is assumed. This rule is used as the USDA Forest Service standard log rule in the Eastern United States.

Log. A primary forest product harvested in long, primarily 8-, 12-, and 16-foot lengths.

Logging residues. The unused merchantable portion of growing-stock trees cut or destroyed during logging operations.

Merchantable portion. That portion of live trees 5.0 inches d.b.h. and larger between a 1-foot stump and a minimum 4.0-inch top d.o.b. on the central stem. That portion of primary forks from the point of occurrence to a minimum 4.0-inch top d.o.b. is included.

Merchantable volume. Solid-wood volume in the merchantable portion of live trees.

Noncommercial species. Tree species of typically small size, poor form, or inferior quality that normally do not develop into trees suitable for industrial wood products.

Nonforest land. Land that has never supported forests and land formerly forested where timber production is precluded by development for other uses.

Nongrowing-stock sources. The net volume removed from the nongrowing-stock portions of poletimber and sawtimber trees (stumps, tops, limbs, cull sections of central stem) and from any portion of a rough, rotten, sapling, dead, or nonforest tree.

Other forest land. Forest land other than timberland and productive reserved forest land. It includes available and reserved forest land that is incapable of producing annually 20 cubic feet per acre of industrial wood under natural conditions because of adverse site conditions such as sterile soils, dry climate, poor drainage, high elevation, steepness, or rockiness.

Other products. A miscellaneous category of roundwood products, e.g., cooperage, excelsior, shingles, and mill residue byproducts (charcoal, bedding, mulch, etc.).

Other removals. The growing-stock volume of trees removed from the inventory by cultural operations such as timber stand improvement, land clearing, and other changes in land use, resulting in the removal of the trees from timberland.

Other sources. (See: Nongrowing-stock sources.)

Poletimber-size trees. Softwoods 5.0 to 8.9 inches d.b.h. and hardwoods 5.0 to 10.9 inches d.b.h.

Posts, poles, and pilings. Roundwood products milled (cut or peeled) into standard sizes (lengths and circumferences) to be put in the ground to provide vertical and lateral support in buildings, foundations, utility lines, and fences. May also include nonindustrial (unmilled) products.

Primary wood-using plants. Industries that convert roundwood products (saw logs, veneer logs, pulpwood, etc.) into primary wood products, such as lumber, veneer or sheathing, and wood pulp.

Pulpwood. A roundwood product that will be reduced to individual wood fibers by chemical or mechanical means. The fibers are used to make a broad generic group of pulp products that includes paper products, as well as chipboard, fiberboard, insulating board, and paperboard.

Rotten trees. Live trees of commercial species not containing at least one 12-foot saw log, or two noncontiguous saw logs, each 8 feet or longer, now or prospectively, primarily because of rot or missing sections, and with less than one-third of the gross board-foot tree volume in sound material.

Rough trees. Live trees of commercial species not containing at least one 12-foot saw log, or two noncontiguous saw logs, each 8 feet or longer, now or prospectively, primarily because of roughness, poor form, splits, and cracks, and with less than one-third of the gross board-foot tree volume in sound material; and live trees of noncommercial species.

Roundwood (roundwood logs). Logs, bolts, or other round sections cut from trees for industrial manufacture or consumer uses.

Roundwood chipped. Any timber cut primarily for industrial manufacture, delivered to nonpulpmills, chipped, and then sold to pulpmills for use as fiber. Includes tops, jump sections, whole trees, and pulpwood sticks.

Roundwood product drain. That portion of total drain used for a product.

Roundwood products. Any primary product, such as lumber, poles, pilings, pulp, or fuelwood that is produced from roundwood.

Salvable dead trees. Standing or downed dead trees that were formerly growing stock and considered merchantable. Trees must be at least 5.0 inches d.b.h. to qualify.

Saplings. Live trees 1.0 to 5.0 inches d.b.h.

Saw log. A roundwood product, usually 8 feet in length or longer, processed into a variety of sawn products such as lumber, cants, pallets, railroad ties, and timbers.

Saw-log portion. The part of the bole of sawtimber trees between a 1-foot stump and the saw-log top.

Saw-log top. The point on the bole of sawtimber trees above which a conventional saw log cannot be produced. The minimum saw-log top is 7.0 inches d.o.b. for softwoods and 9.0 inches d.o.b. for hardwoods.

Sawtimber-size trees. Softwoods 9.0 inches d.b.h. and larger and hardwoods 11.0 inches d.b.h. and larger.

Sawtimber volume. Growing-stock volume in the saw-log portion of sawtimber-sized trees in board feet (International 1/4-inch rule).

Seedlings. Trees <1.0 inch d.b.h. and >1 foot tall for hardwoods, >6 inches tall for softwood, and >0.5 inch in diameter at ground level for longleaf pine.

Softwoods. Coniferous trees, usually evergreen, having leaves that are needles or scalelike.

Standard cord. A unit of measure applied to roundwood, usually bolts or split wood. It is a stack of wood 4 feet high, 4 feet wide, and 8 feet long encompassing 128 cubic feet of wood, bark, and air space. This usually translates to approximately 75.0 to 81.0 cubic feet of solid wood for pulpwood, because pulpwood is more uniform.

Standard unit. A unit measure applied to roundwood timber products. Board feet (International 1/4-inch rule) is the standard unit used for saw logs and veneer; cords are used for pulpwood, composite panel, and fuelwood; hundred pieces for poles; thousand pieces for posts; and thousand cubic feet for all other miscellaneous forest products.

Timberland. Forest land capable of producing 20 cubic feet of industrial wood per acre per year and not withdrawn from timber utilization.

Timber product output. The total volume of roundwood products from all sources plus the volume of byproducts recovered from mill residues (equals roundwood product drain).

Timber products. Roundwood products and byproducts.

Timber removals. The total volume of trees removed from the timberland inventory by harvesting, cultural operations such as stand improvement, land clearing, or changes in land use. (Note: Includes roundwood products, logging residues, and other removals.)

Tree. Woody plant having one erect perennial stem or trunk at least 3 inches d.b.h., a more or less definitely formed crown of foliage, and a height of at least 13 feet (at maturity).

Upper-stem portion. The part of the main stem of sawtimber trees above the saw-log top and the minimum top diameter of 4.0 inches outside bark, or to the point where the main stem breaks into limbs.

Utilization studies. Studies conducted on active logging operations to develop factors for merchantable portions of trees left in the woods (logging residues), logging damage, and utilization of the unmerchantable portion of growing-stock trees and nongrowing-stock trees.

Veneer log. A roundwood product either rotary cut, sliced, stamped, or sawn into a variety of veneer products such as plywood, finished panels, veneer sheets, or sheathing.

Weight. A unit of measure for mill residues, expressed as oven-dry tons (2,000 oven-dry pounds).

Appendix

Index of Tables

Table A.1—Harvest and utilization volume by species group, source, and volume type, Florida, 2008

Species group and source	Total tree volume	Growing stock						Nongrowing stock				
			Saw log		Upper stem				Stumps		Tops/limbs	
		Total	Utilized	Not utilized	Utilized	Not utilized	Total	Utilized	Not utilized	Utilized	Not utilized
							cubic feet					
Softwood												
Sawtimber	22,510.69	19,614.62	16,778.02	972.66	1,489.17	374.77	2,896.07	364.01	802.42	139.41	1,590.23
Poletimber	5,430.08	4,396.52	—	—	4,330.85	65.67	1,033.56	179.75	148.38	434.99	270.44
Total	27,940.77	24,011.14	16,778.02	972.66	5,820.02	440.44	3,929.63	543.76	950.80	574.40	1,860.67
Hardwood												
Sawtimber	10,104.91	8,503.80	6,519.31	747.06	551.09	686.34	1,601.11	130.51	306.34	76.37	1,087.89
Poletimber	2,109.55	1,662.45	—	—	1,552.57	109.88	447.10	61.88	77.52	134.47	173.23
Total	12,214.46	10,166.25	6,519.31	747.06	2,103.66	796.22	2,048.21	192.39	383.86	210.84	1,261.12

— = no sample for the cell.

Table A.2—Volume of softwood growing stock by product and utilization for sawtimber and poletimber, Florida, 2008

Product	Total volume utilized	Growing stock			Nongrowing stock utilized	Saw-log portion			
		Total	Utilized	Not utilized		Total	Utilized	Cull utilized	Not utilized
					cubic feet				
Saw logs	8,239.73	8,619.52	7,967.30	652.22	272.43	6,939.64	6,436.21	354.36	149.07
Veneer logs	5,813.53	5,931.09	5,664.82	266.27	148.71	5,502.79	5,345.52	153.57	3.69
Composite panels	458.77	394.72	381.80	12.92	76.97	17.58	14.71	2.87	—
Pulpwood	3,013.80	2,764.11	2,684.06	80.05	329.74	624.28	587.14	37.14	—
Poles/pilings	2,158.33	2,230.95	2,099.79	131.16	58.54	1,996.57	1,901.19	95.38	—
Fence posts	576.82	534.37	522.44	11.93	54.38	130.67	126.41	4.26	—
Fuelwood	212.58	177.72	175.31	2.41	37.27	9.28	8.07	1.21	—
Mulch	3,242.61	3,358.65	3,102.51	256.14	140.10	2,529.89	2,358.77	-30.67	201.79
Total	23,716.17	24,011.14	22,598.03	1,413.10	1,118.14	17,750.70	16,778.02	618.12	354.55

Numbers in rows and columns may not sum to totals due to rounding.

— = no sample for the cell.

Table A.3—Percent of overutilization and underutilization for softwood growing stock by product for sawtimber and poletimber, Florida, 2008

Product	Overutilization		Underutilization		Saw-log portion		
	Growing stock utilized/ total volume utilized	Nongrowing stock utilized/ total volume utilized	Growing stock utilized/total growing-stock volume	Growing stock not utilized/ total growing-stock volume	Saw log utilized/total saw-log volume	Cull utilized/ total saw-log volume	Saw log not utilized/ total saw-log volume
	percent						
Saw logs	96.69	3.31	92.43	7.57	92.75	5.11	2.15
Veneer logs	97.44	2.56	95.51	4.49	97.14	2.79	0.07
Composite panels	83.22	16.78	96.73	3.27	83.67	16.33	—
Pulpwood	89.06	10.94	97.10	2.90	94.05	5.95	—
Poles/pilings	97.29	2.71	94.12	5.88	95.22	4.78	—
Fence posts	90.57	9.43	97.77	2.23	96.74	3.26	—
Fuelwood	82.46	17.54	98.64	1.36	86.96	13.04	—
Mulch	95.68	4.32	92.37	7.63	93.24	-1.21	7.98
All products	95.29	4.71	94.11	5.89	94.52	3.48	2.00

— = no sample for the cell.

Table A.4—Volume of softwood growing stock by product and utilization for sawtimber, Florida, 2008

Product	Total volume utilized	Growing stock			Nongrowing stock utilized	Saw-log portion			
		Total	Utilized	Not utilized		Total	Utilized	Cull utilized	Not utilized
					cubic feet				
Saw logs	7,362.24	7,800.90	7,155.62	645.28	206.62	6,939.64	6,436.21	354.36	149.07
Veneer logs	5,732.80	5,856.27	5,591.00	265.27	141.80	5,502.79	5,345.52	153.57	3.69
Composite panels	21.46	22.76	19.89	2.87	1.57	17.58	14.71	2.87	—
Pulpwood	735.98	753.54	709.27	44.27	26.71	624.28	587.14	37.14	—
Poles/pilings	2,134.68	2,209.14	2,077.98	131.16	56.70	1,996.57	1,901.19	95.38	—
Fence posts	167.95	165.90	156.23	9.67	11.72	130.67	126.41	4.26	—
Fuelwood	12.65	13.44	12.23	1.21	0.42	9.28	8.07	1.21	—
Mulch	2,602.84	2,792.67	2,544.97	247.70	57.87	2,529.89	2,358.77	-30.67	201.79
Total	18,770.60	19,614.62	18,267.19	1,347.43	503.41	17,750.70	16,778.02	618.12	354.55

Numbers in rows and columns may not sum to totals due to rounding.

— = no sample for the cell.

Table A.5—Percent of overutilization and underutilization for softwood growing stock by product for sawtimber, Florida, 2008

Product	Overutilization		Underutilization		Saw-log portion		
	Growing stock utilized/ total volume utilized	Nongrowing stock utilized/ total volume utilized	Growing stock utilized/total growing-stock volume	Growing stock not utilized/ total growing-stock volume	Saw log utilized/total saw-log volume	Cull utilized/ total saw-log volume	Saw log not utilized/ total saw-log volume
	percent						
Saw logs	97.19	2.81	91.73	8.27	92.75	5.11	2.15
Veneer logs	97.53	2.47	95.47	4.53	97.14	2.79	0.07
Composite panels	92.68	7.32	87.39	12.61	83.67	16.33	—
Pulpwood	96.37	3.63	94.13	5.87	94.05	5.95	—
Poles/pilings	97.34	2.66	94.06	5.94	95.22	4.78	—
Fence posts	93.02	6.98	94.17	5.83	96.74	3.26	—
Fuelwood	96.68	3.32	91.00	9.00	86.96	13.04	—
Mulch	97.78	2.22	91.13	8.87	93.24	-1.21	7.98
All products	97.32	2.68	93.13	6.87	94.52	3.48	2.00

— = no sample for the cell.

Table A.6—Volume of softwood growing stock by product and utilization for poletimber, Florida, 2008

Product	Total volume utilized	Growing stock			Nongrowing stock utilized
		Total	Utilized	Not utilized	
	cubic feet				
Saw logs	877.49	818.62	811.68	6.94	65.81
Veneer logs	80.73	74.82	73.82	1.00	6.91
Composite panels	437.31	371.96	361.91	10.05	75.40
Pulpwood	2,277.82	2,010.57	1,974.79	35.78	303.03
Poles/pilings	23.65	21.81	21.81	—	1.84
Fence posts	408.87	368.47	366.21	2.26	42.66
Fuelwood	199.93	164.28	163.08	1.20	36.85
Mulch	639.77	565.98	557.54	8.44	82.23
Total	4,945.57	4,396.51	4,330.84	65.67	614.73

Numbers in rows and columns may not sum to totals due to rounding.
— = no sample for the cell.

Table A.7—Percent of overutilization and underutilization for softwood growing stock by product for poletimber, Florida, 2008

| | Overutilization | | Underutilization | |
Product	Growing stock utilized/ total volume utilized	Nongrowing stock utilized/ total volume utilized	Growing stock utilized/total growing-stock volume	Growing stock not utilized/ total growing-stock volume
	percent			
Saw logs	92.50	7.50	99.15	0.85
Veneer logs	91.44	8.56	98.66	1.34
Composite panels	82.76	17.24	97.30	2.70
Pulpwood	86.70	13.30	98.22	1.78
Poles/pilings	92.22	7.78	100.00	—
Fence posts	89.57	10.43	99.39	0.61
Fuelwood	81.57	18.43	99.27	0.73
Mulch	87.15	12.85	98.51	1.49
All products	87.57	12.43	98.51	1.49

— = no sample for the cell.

Table A.8—Volume of softwood cull by product and utilization, Florida, 2008

| | | Nongrowing stock | | | |
| | Total volume utilized | | Merchantable | | |
Product		Total	Utilized	Not utilized	Unmerchantable utilized
	cubic feet				
Saw logs	—	—	—	—	—
Veneer logs	—	—	—	—	—
Composite panels	—	—	—	—	—
Pulpwood	58.61	57.04	56.78	0.26	1.83
Poles/pilings	—	—	—	—	—
Fence posts	—	—	—	—	—
Fuelwood	27.92	20.64	20.64	0.00	7.28
Mulch	135.30	134.59	133.97	0.62	1.33
Total	221.83	212.27	211.39	0.88	10.44

Numbers in rows and columns may not sum to totals due to rounding.

— = no sample for the cell.

Table A.9—Percent of overutilization and underutilization for softwood cull by product, Florida, 2008

Product	Overutilization		Underutilization	
	Merchantable utilized/ total volume utilized	Unmerchantable utilized/ total volume utilized	Merchantable utilized/total merchantable volume	Merchantable not utilized/total merchantable volume
	percent			
Saw logs	—	—	—	—
Veneer logs	—	—	—	—
Composite panels	—	—	—	—
Pulpwood	96.88	3.12	99.54	0.46
Poles/pilings	—	—	—	—
Fence posts	—	—	—	—
Fuelwood	73.93	26.07	100.00	—
Mulch	99.02	0.98	99.54	0.46
All products	95.29	4.71	99.59	0.41

— = no sample for the cell.

Table A.10—Volume of hardwood growing stock by product and utilization for sawtimber and poletimber, Florida, 2008

Product	Total volume utilized	Growing stock			Nongrowing stock utilized	Saw-log portion			
		Total	Utilized	Not utilized		Total	Utilized	Cull utilized	Not utilized
					cubic feet				
Saw logs	6,077.95	7,285.63	5,963.94	1,321.69	114.01	6,211.11	5,528.49	682.62	—
Veneer logs	—	—	—	—	—	—	—	—	—
Composite panels	—	—	—	—	—	—	—	—	—
Pulpwood	2,078.37	2,183.53	1,963.31	220.22	115.06	757.69	693.24	64.45	—
Poles/pilings	—	—	—	—	—	—	—	—	—
Fence posts	—	—	—	—	—	—	—	—	—
Fuelwood	858.01	685.11	685.11	—	172.90	297.58	297.58	—	—
Mulch	11.89	11.99	10.62	1.37	1.27	—	—	—	—
Total	9,026.22	10,166.25	8,622.98	1,543.28	403.24	7,266.38	6,519.31	747.07	—

Numbers in rows and columns may not sum to totals due to rounding.

— = no sample for the cell.

Table A.11—Percent of overutilization and underutilization for hardwood growing stock by product for sawtimber and poletimber, Florida, 2008

	Overutilization		Underutilization		Saw-log portion		
Product	Growing stock utilized/ total volume utilized	Nongrowing stock utilized/ total volume utilized	Growing stock utilized/total growing-stock volume	Growing stock not utilized/ total growing-stock volume	Saw log utilized/ total saw-log volume	Cull utilized/ total saw-log volume	Saw log not utilized/total saw-log volume
				percent			
Saw logs	98.12	1.88	81.86	18.14	89.01	10.99	—
Veneer logs	—	—	—	—	—	—	—
Composite panels	—	—	—	—	—	—	—
Pulpwood	94.46	5.54	89.91	10.09	91.49	8.51	—
Poles/pilings	—	—	—	—	—	—	—
Fence posts	—	—	—	—	—	—	—
Fuelwood	79.85	20.15	100.00	—	100.00	—	—
Mulch	89.32	10.68	88.57	11.43	—	—	—
All products	95.53	4.47	84.82	15.18	89.72	10.28	—

— = no sample for the cell.

Table A.12—Volume of hardwood growing stock by product and utilization for sawtimber, Florida, 2008

		Growing stock				Saw-log portion			
Product	Total volume utilized	Total	Utilized	Not utilized	Nongrowing stock utilized	Total	Utilized	Cull utilized	Not utilized
					cubic feet				
Saw logs	5,961.40	7,162.81	5,855.64	1,307.17	105.76	6,211.11	5,528.49	682.62	—
Veneer logs	—	—	—	—	—	—	—	—	—
Composite panels	—	—	—	—	—	—	—	—	—
Pulpwood	877.30	980.30	854.07	126.23	23.23	757.69	693.24	64.45	—
Poles/pilings	—	—	—	—	—	—	—	—	—
Fence posts	—	—	—	—	—	—	—	—	—
Fuelwood	438.59	360.70	360.70	—	77.89	297.58	297.58	—	—
Mulch	—	—	—	—	—	—	—	—	—
Total	7,277.29	8,503.81	7,070.41	1,433.40	206.88	7,266.38	6,519.31	747.07	—

Numbers in rows and columns may not sum to totals due to rounding.

— = no sample for the cell.

Table A.13—Percent of overutilization and underutilization for hardwood growing stock by product for sawtimber, Florida, 2008

Product	Overutilization		Underutilization		Saw-log portion		
	Growing stock utilized/ total volume utilized	Nongrowing stock utilized/ total volume utilized	Growing stock utilized/total growing-stock volume	Growing stock not utilized/ total growing-stock volume	Saw log utilized/ total saw-log volume	Cull utilized/ total saw-log volume	Saw log not utilized/ total saw-log volume
	percent						
Saw logs	98.23	1.77	81.75	18.25	89.01	10.99	—
Veneer logs	—	—	—	—	—	—	—
Composite panels	—	—	—	—	—	—	—
Pulpwood	97.35	2.65	87.12	12.88	91.49	8.51	—
Poles/pilings	—	—	—	—	—	—	—
Fence posts	—	—	—	—	—	—	—
Fuelwood	82.24	17.76	100.00	—	100.00	—	—
Mulch	—	—	—	—	—	—	—
All products	97.16	2.84	83.14	16.86	89.72	10.28	—

— = no sample for the cell.

Table A.14—Volume of hardwood growing stock by product and utilization for poletimber, Florida, 2008

Product	Total volume utilized	Growing stock			Nongrowing stock utilized
		Total	Utilized	Not utilized	
	cubic feet				
Saw logs	116.55	122.82	108.30	14.52	8.25
Veneer logs	—	—	—	—	—
Composite panels	—	—	—	—	—
Pulpwood	1,201.07	1,203.23	1,109.24	93.99	91.83
Poles/pilings	—	—	—	—	—
Fence posts	—	—	—	—	—
Fuelwood	419.42	324.41	324.41	—	95.01
Mulch	11.89	11.99	10.62	1.37	1.27
Total	1,748.93	1,662.45	1,552.57	109.88	196.36

Numbers in rows and columns may not sum to totals due to rounding.

— = no sample for the cell.

Table A.15—Percent of overutilization and underutilization for hardwood growing stock by product for poletimber, Florida, 2008

Product	Overutilization		Underutilization	
	Growing stock utilized/ total volume utilized	Nongrowing stock utilized/ total volume utilized	Growing stock utilized/total growing-stock volume	Growing stock not utilized/ total growing-stock volume
	percent			
Saw logs	92.92	7.08	88.18	11.82
Veneer logs	—	—	—	—
Composite panels	—	—	—	—
Pulpwood	92.35	7.65	92.19	7.81
Poles/pilings	—	—	—	—
Fence posts	—	—	—	—
Fuelwood	77.35	22.65	100.00	—
Mulch	89.32	10.68	88.57	11.43
All products	88.77	11.23	93.39	6.61

— = no sample for the cell.

Table A.16—Volume of hardwood cull by product and utilization, Florida, 2008

Product	Total volume utilized	Nongrowing stock			
		Merchantable			Unmerchantable utilized
		Total	Utilized	Not utilized	
		cubic feet			
Saw logs	—	—	—	—	—
Veneer logs	—	—	—	—	—
Composite panels	—	—	—	—	—
Pulpwood	343.31	322.63	306.76	15.87	36.55
Poles/pilings	—	—	—	—	—
Fence posts	—	—	—	—	—
Fuelwood	—	—	—	—	—
Mulch	32.80	30.59	29.52	1.07	3.28
Total	376.11	353.22	336.28	16.94	39.83

Numbers in rows and columns may not sum to totals due to rounding.

— = no sample for the cell.

Table A.17—Percent of overutilization and underutilization for hardwood cull by product, Florida, 2008

Product	Overutilization		Underutilization	
	Merchantable utilized/total volume utilized	Unmerchantable utilized/total volume utilized	Merchantable utilized/total merchantable volume	Merchantable not utilized/total merchantable volume
	percent			
Saw logs	—	—	—	—
Veneer logs	—	—	—	—
Composite panels	—	—	—	—
Pulpwood	89.35	10.65	95.08	4.92
Poles/pilings	—	—	—	—
Fence posts	—	—	—	—
Fuelwood	—	—	—	—
Mulch	90.00	10.00	96.50	3.50
All products	89.41	10.59	95.20	4.80

— = no sample for the cell.